AF454729

the
SINS & WINS
of
Dr. Anthony
Giannoumis
Sumita
Kunashakaran
Lisa
Haynes

INCLUSIVE Design

A blueprint to designing for diversity

I've f*cked up so you don't have to!

The inclusion journey can seem daunting.

Allow us to be your guides!

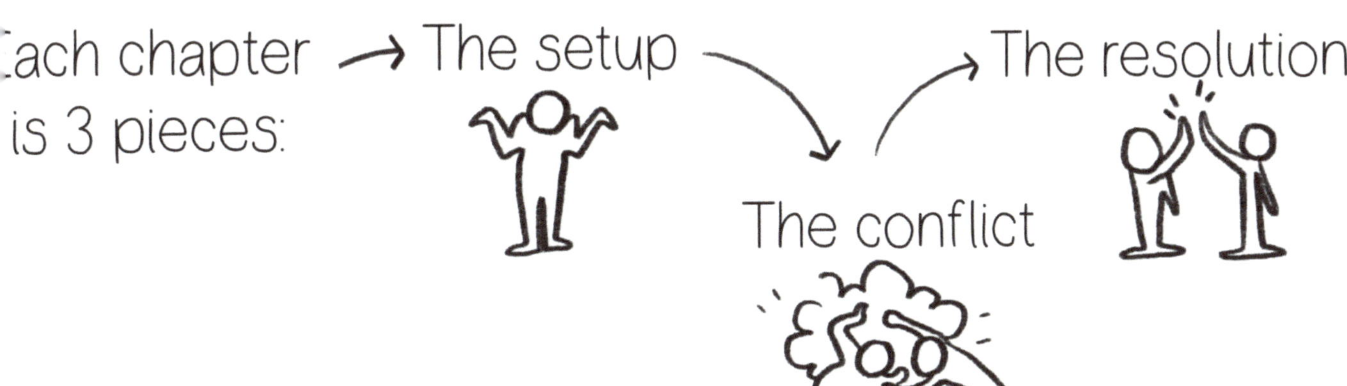
Each chapter
is 3 pieces:
The setup
The conflict
The resolution

At the end of each chapter, look for my "Su's clues"
Learn to put your principles into practice!

THE "NORMAL" PERSON

Elaine buys a printer so she can print a picture of her grandson.

She tries and tries to get it to work, but grows so frustrated she smashes it against the wall.

DESIGN FOR ALL

If a printer works for Elaine, it'll work better for everyone.

Inclusive design is necessary for some & awesome for everyone.

Make inclusive design work for your workplace. Design products (and work spaces!) customized for one-size-fits-one, not one-size-fits-all.

THE INNOVATOR

I'm going to
make a phone
for blind people!

Jeremy is an innovator.
He invented a phone for blind people.

Have you talked to anyone who is blind about your idea?
Money please!
No, but i'm a genius! it's a great idea! i'm going to help so many people!

He pitches his idea to investors.

TALK TO YOUR USERS

So? Great idea, am I right?
Can I pet that dog?
Why would we want a separate phone?
This is not helpful.
Don't pet me... I'm a service dog!

Jeremy meets with a disabled person's organization and realizes he made a mistake.

Innovation needs collaboration

Nothing about us without us! And everything is about us! Ensure your spaces are welcoming and open to all, and question your assumptions.

THE EQUAL OPPORTUNITY

Johnny's McBusiness
WARNING
People with BLUE shirts not allowed
equal rights!
unfair!!

Johnny is on the wrong side of history.

Johnny's McBusiness
EVERYONE IS WELCOME!
WTF do you mean everyone??!

He makes a change, but overlooks a lot of people.

DESIGN FOR ACCESSIBILITY

Johnny's McBusiness
WE REALLY
MEAN
EVERYONE
THIS TIME

Equality is about more than stopping discrimination. It's about giving everyone an equal chance in life.

Equality is accessibility

Working together creates impact. Trying not to exclude anyone might seem daunting, but exploring your world together can give you a renewed perspective!

THE "SAFE" SPACE

What if it's a box made out of diamonds??
..or a round box?
Oh! We should put a box in a box!
Let's think outside the box!
What if it's not a box at all? ...no that's a silly idea...

Henry and his team are excited to come up with new ideas for a product.

Good job!
Amazing!
Great idea!!
This is a terrible idea
What about a box made out of cardboard!

Helen has amazing insights but doesn't
feel comfortable sharing them.

MAKE SPACE FOR EVERYONE

Well, I think maybe it's not a box at all, and the cardboard idea just doesn't seem innovative
Brilliant!
and I have some other ideas, but I can send them on email!
Helen, what do you think?
I can't wait to get her email!
Oh wow!!

Henry sees that Helen's quiet so he creates space for her to contribute if she wants to.

Creating space makes a space creative.

Creating safe spaces also means creating "brave spaces" where everyone feels empowered to make their voice heard. Try creative alternatives like writing, singing or dancing to give everyone a chance to express themselves!

THE DIGITALIZER

A clinic decides to switch their appointment system to a mobile app.

We are empowering you!
The app is not accessible!
My kids don't speak English?
I don't have a smartphone...

But it doesn't inform its patients ahead of time or provide alternatives.

CREATE CHANNELS OF CONNECTION

Here are our options for our patients.
MOBILE APP
PHONE CALL
VISIT OUR CLINIC

A welcoming environment respects and addresses diversity.

Diverse needs need diverse choices.

By integrating input before decisions, accessible services can empower lives.

THE PERFORMANCE REVIEWER

Paul! You did a great job during golf today! Here's a promotion!

Yay!

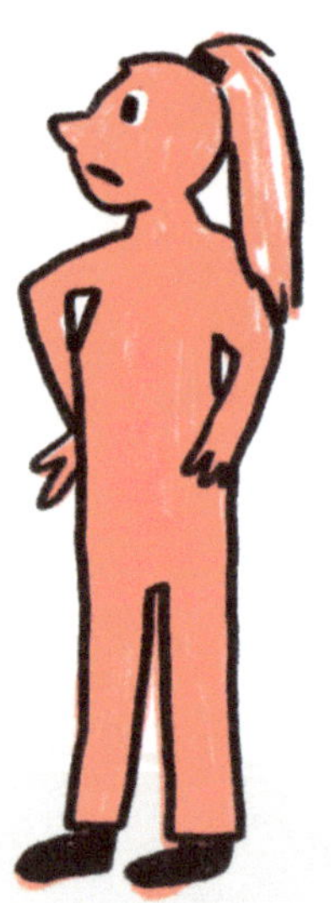

But I didn't even get invited?

John rolls out a new way to review employees' work.

I quit!
But why? You do such a good job?

People are very unhappy with the new system, and it makes many feel left out.

MAKE PERFORMANCE REVIEWS PARTICIPATORY

We need a new evaluation system!
Any ideas?
A different schedule for parents
No golf network!
I love remote work
How do we measure soft skills?

Time to revisit the design of the system by involving employees from diverse backgrounds.

Equity in the workplace is ethical, and essential!

True equity in design should
never be an after-thought!
Consider all perspectives from
the start

THE TEAMBUILDER

Let's all go skydiving! It'll be fun!
But no one asked us what we wanted to do?
I did all the research and this was the best idea!

Amy works in a company, but doesn't engage staff in community initiatives.

Why did no one sign up?
I can't skydive!
I'm afraid of heights!
Will my wheelchair also go flying?!
Maybe everyone is not keen to be part of the team?

Despite offering various programmes, sign-ups remain low.

CREATE COMMUNITY

We can do a picnic!
How about football?
These are all great ideas!
How about a charity drive?

Amy decides on a fun activity with her team.

Inclusivity thrives on innovation!

By involving everyone, a community is built!

The road ahead is yours!

THE
~~END~~
BEGINNING